Winter Dreams

*Obsession, Class & Lost Illusions
beneath the Frost of the
American Dream*

A Modern Translation
Adapted for the Contemporary Reader

F. Scott Fitzgerald

Translated by Tim Zengerink

Table of Contents

Preface
Message to the Reader

Rebuilding the Greatest Library in Human History

Thousands of years ago, the Library of Alexandria was the heart of global knowledge — a sanctuary where the wisdom of every known civilization was gathered and shared freely.

And then, it was lost.

Now, we're rebuilding it — and you are invited to join us.

At the Library of Alexandria, we've set out to make every book available to every person on Earth — not just in print, but in every language, every format, and for every reader.

Here's how we do it:

- **Deluxe Print Editions at True Printing Cost** - Order any book as a high-quality paperback, elegant hardcover, or stunning boxset — and only pay what it costs to print. No markups. No middlemen.
- **Unlimited Access to the Greatest Works** - Enjoy thousands of timeless classics — from Plato to Shakespeare to Tolstoy — in beautiful, modern eBook and audiobook editions. Read and listen without limits — for every reader, everywhere.
- **Modern Translations for Every Language & Dialect** - We're reimagining the classics in clear, accessible language — and translating them into every dialect imaginable. Everyone deserves to understand humanity's greatest ideas.

When you visit **LibraryofAlexandria.com**, you're not just accessing books — you're joining a global movement to restore, preserve, and share the wisdom of civilization.

Join us today at LibraryofAlexandria.com

Together, we'll ensure the light of human wisdom never fades again.

With gratitude,

The Modern Library of Alexandria Team

Visit:
www.libraryofalexandria.com
Or scan the code below:

Introduction

Fitzgerald's Prelude to Gatsby: The American Dream, Class, and Desire

F. Scott Fitzgerald's *Winter Dreams*, first published in *Metropolitan Magazine* in December 1922 and later collected in All the Sad Young Men (1926), is often regarded as a spiritual prelude to his masterpiece *The Great Gatsby*. It is a story that delves into themes of ambition, social aspiration, romantic obsession, and the ultimate disillusionment that accompanies the pursuit of an unattainable ideal. Through the rise and fall of Dexter Green, the protagonist, Fitzgerald crafts a narrative that is at once deeply personal and universally resonant, capturing the fleeting nature of youth, love, and the American Dream.

At its core, *Winter Dreams* is the story of a young man who yearns for a life beyond his modest beginnings. Dexter, the son of a middle-class grocery store owner in Minnesota, is acutely aware of the social hierarchy that separates him from the wealthy elite. From a young age, he is enchanted by the glittering world of privilege and luxury, symbolized most vividly by the character of Judy Jones, a beautiful and capricious young woman who becomes the object of his deepest desires. Judy is not just a romantic interest for Dexter; she represents all that he longs for—wealth, status, and the allure of an unattainable ideal.

Fitzgerald's portrayal of Dexter's obsession with Judy is both poignant and critical. While Judy is undeniably charming and charismatic, she is also shallow and fickle, her beauty masking an emptiness that Dexter refuses to acknowledge until it is too late. His pursuit of her is driven less by genuine love than by the dream she embodies—a dream of rising above his station, of belonging to the glittering world of the privileged few. In this sense, Judy is less a character than a symbol, a personification of Dexter's "winter dreams," those shimmering but ultimately illusory aspirations that drive him forward but leave him empty when they fade.

The title itself, *Winter Dreams*, is deeply evocative, suggesting both the beauty and the transience of dreams. Winter, with its stark landscapes and fleeting moments of brightness, mirrors the tone of the story—a world of fleeting passions, frozen ambitions, and the inevitable thaw that reveals the emptiness beneath. For Dexter, winter is both a season of longing and a metaphor for the cold pursuit of material success. His dreams, like snow, glisten brightly for a time but are destined to melt away.

Fitzgerald's exploration of class in *Winter Dreams* is particularly striking. The story reflects the rigid social divisions of early 20th-century America, where wealth and status often determined one's opportunities and sense of self-worth. Dexter's desire to escape his middle-class background and join the ranks of the elite is not merely a personal ambition but a reflection of the broader American Dream—a dream that promises upward mobility but often exacts a heavy emotional cost. Through Dexter's journey, Fitzgerald critiques the hollowness of this dream, showing how the pursuit of wealth and status can lead to disillusionment and a loss of true identity.

One of the most powerful aspects of *Winter Dreams* is its mood of nostalgia and melancholy. Fitzgerald, who often infused his stories with autobiographical elements, was deeply familiar with the pain of lost love and unfulfilled dreams. In many ways, Dexter's yearning for Judy mirrors Fitzgerald's own romantic and social ambitions, particularly his pursuit of Zelda Sayre, the Southern belle who would become his wife and muse. Like Dexter, Fitzgerald was captivated by beauty, wealth, and the promise of a glittering social life, but he also understood the fleeting and often destructive nature of such desires.

Reading Winter Dreams today, one cannot help but draw parallels to *The Great Gatsby*, which Fitzgerald would publish just a few years later. Both stories feature a self-made man who is driven by an unattainable ideal, and both highlight the gap between illusion and reality. In Dexter, we see a precursor to Jay Gatsby—a man who builds his life around a dream that ultimately crumbles, leaving him disillusioned and alone. Yet while Gatsby's dream is rooted in the past, Dexter's "winter dreams" are more abstract, tied not only to love but to a broader longing for meaning and permanence in a transient world.

Themes of Love, Illusion, and Disillusionment

One of the central themes of *Winter Dreams* is the tension between reality and illusion. For Dexter, Judy Jones is less a real person than a dream, an idealized vision of beauty and success that he chases at the expense of everything else. This theme is most evident in the way Dexter's perception of Judy changes over time. In their youth, Judy is the embodiment of charm and perfection, but as the years pass, her beauty fades, and Dexter is forced to confront the reality that the dream he cherished was never as perfect as he imagined. This realization is devastating, not just because he loses Judy, but because it shatters the ideal that has guided his life.

Fitzgerald's treatment of love in this story is deeply cynical, yet profoundly true. He suggests that much of what we call "love" is often driven by projection and idealization rather than genuine understanding of the other person. Dexter never truly knows Judy; he is in love with what she represents—a life of luxury, youth, and unattainable perfection. Judy, for her part, is portrayed as a woman who wields her beauty like a weapon, captivating men but offering little in the way of depth or sincerity. In this dynamic, Fitzgerald critiques the shallow values of a society that prizes appearances over substance.

The theme of disillusionment runs throughout the story, culminating in the heartbreaking final scenes where Dexter learns of Judy's decline. By the time he hears of her fate— married to a man who mistreats her, her beauty faded— Dexter has already achieved material success. Yet this success feels hollow, because the dream that once gave his life meaning has vanished. In one of the story's most haunting lines, Fitzgerald writes that "the dream was gone. Something had been taken from him." This sense of loss, of a dream slipping away, is quintessential Fitzgerald, echoing the famous line from *The Great Gatsby* about the "orgastic future that year by year recedes before us."

Class and ambition are also central to the story. Dexter's journey from middle-class obscurity to wealth is a testament to his determination and drive, but it is also a critique of the values that define success in America. His desire to join the ranks of the wealthy is not motivated by a genuine passion for business or achievement, but by a desire to win Judy and prove his worth. In this sense, his success is tainted by its foundation in superficial values, and it ultimately fails to bring him happiness.

Fitzgerald's Style, Symbolism, and Legacy

Fitzgerald's writing in *Winter Dreams* is both lyrical and precise, capturing the beauty of fleeting moments and the inner turmoil of his characters. His use of seasonal imagery—particularly winter—adds a layer of symbolism that deepens the story's themes. Winter, with its cold beauty and inevitable thaw, mirrors Dexter's own emotional journey, from the bright promise of youth to the disillusionment of maturity. The frozen lakes, the sparkling snow, and the changing seasons all serve as metaphors for the impermanence of life and the futility of clinging to dreams that cannot endure.

The character of Dexter Green is one of Fitzgerald's most fully realized protagonists. Ambitious, intelligent, and driven, he is both admirable and deeply flawed. His obsession with Judy blinds him to the possibility of a more genuine and fulfilling life, and his ultimate disillusionment serves as a cautionary tale about the dangers of idealizing both people and dreams. Judy, meanwhile, is a complex and enigmatic figure, representing both the allure and the emptiness of the world Dexter longs to enter. Her beauty is dazzling but transient, a reminder that all things—youth, love, success—are subject to the passage of time.

Winter Dreams has been widely studied for its connections to *The Great Gatsby*, and many critics view it as a kind of "first draft" of the themes that Fitzgerald would later explore more fully in his novel. Both works grapple with the tension between dream and reality, the seductive but destructive power of wealth and beauty, and the longing for a past or an ideal that can never be recaptured. Yet *Winter Dreams* stands on its own as a powerful and haunting story, a testament to Fitzgerald's skill as a short story writer.

The story's enduring relevance lies in its exploration of universal human experiences—ambition, love, loss, and the passage of time. In a world that continues to place a high value on youth, beauty, and material success, Dexter's journey feels as poignant today as it did a century ago. His story is a reminder that the things we chase most fervently are often the most ephemeral, and that true fulfillment comes not from external validation but from a deeper understanding of ourselves and our values.

Winter Dreams

Chapter 1

Some of the caddies were dirt poor and lived in tiny one-room homes with a sickly cow grazing in their front yards, but Dexter Green's father owned the second-best grocery store in Black Bear—the top store was "The Hub," which served the rich folks from Sherry Island—and Dexter only worked as a caddie to earn spending money.

In the fall when the days turned crisp and gray, and the long Minnesota winter closed down like the white lid of a box, Dexter's skis glided over the snow that covered the fairways of the golf course. During these times the countryside filled him with a sense of deep melancholy—it bothered him that the golf course should lie in forced dormancy, visited only by scraggly sparrows throughout the long season. It was also depressing that on the tees where bright colors had fluttered in summer there were now only the barren sand-boxes buried knee-deep in hardened ice. When he crossed the hills the wind blew as cold as misery, and if the sun was shining he trudged with his eyes narrowed against the harsh, flat glare.

In April, winter ended suddenly. The snow melted and flowed down into Black Bear Lake, barely lingering long enough for eager golfers to venture out for the season with their red and black balls. There was no gradual transition, no period of damp splendor—the cold simply vanished.

Dexter understood that something depressing hung over this Northern spring, just as he recognized something magnificent about autumn. Fall made him clench his fists and shake while muttering nonsensical phrases to himself, and he would make sharp, sudden commanding gestures toward imaginary crowds and troops. October filled him with hope that November elevated to a kind of euphoric victory, and in this frame of mind the brief, vivid memories of that summer at Sherry Island became perfect fuel for his fantasies. He transformed into a golf champion and beat Mr. T. A. Hedrick in an incredible match played countless times across the fairways of his mind, a match whose every detail he endlessly modified—sometimes he won with almost ridiculous ease, sometimes he mounted a spectacular comeback from behind. In another scenario, stepping out of a Pierce-Arrow automobile, like Mr. Mortimer Jones, he walked coolly into the lounge of the Sherry Island Golf Club—or perhaps, encircled by an admiring audience, he performed an exhibition of elaborate diving from the springboard of the club raft.... Among those who observed him in amazed silence was Mr. Mortimer Jones.

And one day it happened that Mr. Jones—the man himself, not his ghost—approached Dexter with tears in his eyes and told him that Dexter was the damn best caddy in the club, and wouldn't he reconsider quitting if Mr. Jones made it worth his while, because every other damn caddy in the club lost one ball per hole for him—without fail—

"No, sir," Dexter said with finality, "I don't want to caddy anymore." After a moment of silence, he added: "I'm too old."

"You're not even fourteen yet. Why on earth did you suddenly decide this morning that you wanted to quit? You promised me that next week you'd come with me to the State tournament."

"I decided I was too old."

Dexter turned in his "A Class" badge, picked up the money owed to him from the caddy master, and headed home to Black Bear Village.

"The best caddy I ever saw," shouted Mr. Mortimer Jones over a drink that afternoon. "Never lost a ball! Willing! Intelligent! Quiet! Honest! Grateful!"

The little girl who had done this was eleven—beautifully awkward in the way that girls often are when they're destined to become breathtakingly beautiful in a few years and cause endless heartbreak for countless men. Still, you could already see the spark. There was something mischievous about how her lips curved downward at the corners when she smiled, and in her eyes—God help us all—there was an almost intense, passionate quality. This kind of life force emerges early in such women. It was completely obvious now, radiating through her slender body like an inner light.

She had eagerly arrived at the golf course at nine o'clock with a white-uniformed nurse and five small new golf clubs in a white canvas bag that the nurse was carrying. When Dexter first spotted her, she was standing near the caddy house, looking quite uncomfortable and attempting to hide this by forcing an awkward conversation with her nurse, punctuated by surprising and completely unrelated facial expressions.

"Well, it's definitely a beautiful day, Hilda," Dexter heard her say. She pulled down the corners of her mouth, smiled, and looked around secretly, her eyes briefly landing on Dexter as they moved.

Then to the nurse:

"Well, I suppose there aren't many people out here this morning, are there?"

The smile appeared once more—brilliant, obviously fake—yet persuasive.

"I don't know what we're supposed to do now," said the nurse, looking nowhere in particular.

"Oh, that's all right. I'll fix it up."

Dexter remained completely motionless, his mouth hanging slightly open. He understood that if he stepped forward, she would notice him staring—if he stepped back, he would no longer have a clear view of her face. For a brief moment, he hadn't realized just how young she was. Now he recalled having spotted her multiple times the previous year—wearing bloomers.

Suddenly, without meaning to, he burst into laughter— a brief, sharp laugh. Then, surprised by his own reaction, he spun around and started walking rapidly away.

"Boy!"

Dexter stopped.

"Boy——"

Without a doubt, he was being spoken to. Not only that, but he received that ridiculous smile, that outrageous smile—the memory of which at least a dozen men would carry with them into their middle years.

"Hey kid, do you know where the golf instructor is?"

"He's giving a lesson."

"Well, do you know where the caddy-master is?"

"He hasn't arrived yet this morning."

"Oh." For a moment this confused her. She shifted her weight back and forth from her right foot to her left foot.

"We'd like to get a caddy," said the nurse. "Mrs. Mortimer Jones sent us out to play golf, and we don't know how to do it without getting a caddy."

Here she was interrupted by a threatening look from Miss Jones, which was immediately followed by the smile.

"There aren't any caddies here except me," Dexter told the nurse, "and I have to stay here in charge until the caddy-master arrives."

"Oh."

Miss Jones and her group stepped back, positioning themselves at an appropriate distance from Dexter before launching into an intense argument. The discussion ended with Miss Jones grabbing one of the clubs and slamming it forcefully against the ground. To make her point even more dramatically, she lifted the club again and was preparing to strike the nurse squarely on the chest, but the nurse quickly grabbed the club and wrenched it away from her.

"You damn little mean old thing!" cried Miss Jones wildly.

Another argument broke out. Dexter recognized that the situation contained all the makings of a comedy, and he started to laugh several times, but each time he held back the laughter before it could be heard. He couldn't shake the outrageous belief that the little girl was right to hit the nurse.

The problem was solved when the caddy-master happened to show up, and the nurse immediately asked him for help.

"Miss Jones is supposed to have a young golf caddy, and this boy says he can't go."

"Mr. McKenna told me to wait here until you arrived," Dexter said quickly.

"Well, he's here now." Miss Jones smiled cheerfully at the caddy-master. Then she dropped her bag and walked off with a proud, affected stride toward the first tee.

"Well?" The caddy-master turned to Dexter. "What are you standing there like an idiot for? Go pick up the young lady's clubs."

"I don't think I'll go out today," said Dexter.

"You don't——"

"I think I'll quit."

The magnitude of his choice terrified him. He was a well-liked caddy, and the thirty dollars he made each month during the summer couldn't be earned anywhere else around the lake. However, he had experienced an intense emotional blow, and his distress demanded a forceful and instant release.

It wasn't that straightforward, though. As would happen so often in the years to come, Dexter was unknowingly controlled by his winter dreams.

Chapter 2

Now, naturally, the quality and timing of these winter dreams changed, but their essence stayed the same. They convinced Dexter several years later to skip a business program at the State university—his father, who was doing well financially now, would have covered the costs—in favor of the risky benefit of going to an older and more prestigious university in the East, where his limited money caused him problems. But don't assume, just because his winter dreams initially focused on thoughts about wealthy people, that the boy was simply being a snob. He didn't want to be around glamorous things and glamorous people—he wanted those glamorous things for himself. He often reached for the finest things without understanding why he desired them—and sometimes he encountered the puzzling rejections and restrictions that life throws at us. This story focuses on one of those rejections, not on his entire career.

He made money. It was quite remarkable. After college, he moved to the city that supplied Black Bear Lake with its wealthy visitors. By the time he was just twenty-three and had been there less than two years, people were already saying: "Now there's a young man—" Around him, the sons of rich men were selling bonds with little success, or recklessly investing their inheritances, or struggling through the twenty-four volumes of the "George Washington Commercial Course," but Dexter borrowed a thousand dollars based on his college degree and his persuasive manner, and purchased a partnership in a laundry.

It was a small laundry when he entered it, but Dexter specialized in learning how the English cleaned fine woolen golf stockings without causing them to shrink, and within a year he was serving the clientele that wore knickerbockers. Men were demanding that their Shetland socks and sweaters be taken to his laundry just as they had demanded a caddy who could locate golf balls. Shortly afterward, he was also handling their wives' undergarments—and operating five locations in different areas of the city. Before he reached twenty-seven, he owned the largest chain of laundries in his region of the country. It was at that point that he sold his business and moved to New York. But the portion of his story that interests us returns to the time when he was achieving his first major success.

When he turned twenty-three, Mr. Hart—one of those gray-haired men who enjoy saying "Now there's a boy"— gave him a guest membership to the Sherry Island Golf Club for a weekend. He signed his name in the register one day, and that afternoon he played golf in a foursome with Mr. Hart, Mr. Sandwood, and Mr. T. A. Hedrick. He didn't think it was necessary to mention that he had once carried Mr. Hart's golf bag over these very same links, and that he knew every sand trap and water hazard with his eyes closed—but he caught himself looking at the four caddies who followed them around, searching for a spark or movement that would remind him of his former self, something that might bridge the distance between who he was now and who he used to be.

It was a strange day, cut sharply by brief, recognizable moments. One moment he felt like an intruder—the next he was struck by the overwhelming sense of superiority he experienced toward Mr. T. A. Hedrick, who was tedious and no longer even a decent golfer.

Then, because Mr. Hart lost a ball near the fifteenth green, something enormous happened. While they searched through the thick rough grass, a clear shout of "Fore!" rang out from behind a hill behind them. As they all quickly turned from their search, a bright new ball suddenly flew over the hill and struck Mr. T. A. Hedrick in the stomach.

"Good God!" exclaimed Mr. T. A. Hedrick, "they should remove some of these insane women from the golf course. This is becoming absolutely ridiculous."

A head and a voice appeared together over the hill:

"Do you mind if we go through?"

"You punched me in the stomach!" Mr. Hedrick exclaimed frantically.

"Did I?" The girl walked toward the group of men. "I'm sorry. I shouted 'Fore!'"

Her eyes casually looked at each of the men—then searched the fairway for her ball.

"Did I bounce into the rough?"

It was impossible to tell whether this question was sincere or spiteful. Within moments, though, she made her intentions clear, because when her partner appeared over the hill she called out happily:

"Here I am! I would have continued on the green except that I hit something."

As she positioned herself for a short mashie shot, Dexter studied her carefully. She was dressed in a blue gingham outfit, trimmed at the neckline and shoulders with white edging that highlighted her tanned skin. The exaggerated quality, the gauntness, that had made her intense eyes and downward-curved mouth look ridiculous when she was eleven, had vanished. She was strikingly beautiful. The color in her cheeks was concentrated like pigment in a painting—it wasn't a bright flush, but rather a kind of shifting and fevered warmth, so subtle that it appeared ready to fade and vanish at any second. This coloring and the expressiveness of her mouth created a constant sense of change, of vibrant energy, of intense passion—only partly counterbalanced by the melancholy richness of her eyes.

She swung her golf club impatiently and without interest, sending the ball into a sand trap on the other side of the green. With a quick, insincere smile and a careless "Thank you!" she went on after it.

"That Judy Jones!" Mr. Hedrick commented on the next tee as they waited for several moments for her to play ahead. "All she needs is to be disciplined for six months and then married off to an old-fashioned cavalry captain."

"My God, she's beautiful!" said Mr. Sandwood, who was just over thirty.

"Good-looking!" Mr. Hedrick said with contempt, "she always looks like she's begging to be kissed! Batting those big doe-eyes at every young man in town!"

It was unclear whether Mr. Hedrick meant to refer to the maternal instinct.

"She would play pretty good golf if she tried," said Mr. Sandwood.

"She has no form," Mr. Hedrick said solemnly.

"She has a nice figure," said Mr. Sandwood.

"Thank goodness she doesn't hit the ball any harder," said Mr. Hart, winking at Dexter.

Later that afternoon, the sun set in a wild swirl of gold, blues, and scarlets, leaving behind the dry, rustling night typical of Western summers. Dexter watched from the Golf Club's veranda, observing the gentle ripples on the water in the light breeze, which looked like silver molasses beneath the harvest moon. Then the moon seemed to press a finger to her lips, and the lake transformed into a clear, pale, and peaceful pool. Dexter changed into his bathing suit and swam out to the most distant raft, where he lay dripping on the wet canvas of the diving board.

There was a fish leaping from the water and a star twinkling overhead while the lights surrounding the lake sparkled brightly. Across the water on a shadowy peninsula, someone was playing piano melodies from the previous summer and summers long past—tunes from "Chin-Chin" and "The Count of Luxemburg" and "The Chocolate Soldier"—and since the sound of piano music drifting across water had always struck Dexter as beautiful, he remained completely still and listened.

The song the piano was playing at that moment had been cheerful and popular five years earlier when Dexter was a college sophomore. They had played it at a dance once when he couldn't afford the luxury of attending dances, and he had stood outside the gymnasium listening. The sound of the melody triggered a kind of euphoria in him, and it was through this euphoria that he experienced what was happening to him now. It was a feeling of deep appreciation, a sense that, for once, he was perfectly in harmony with life and that everything around him was glowing with a brilliance and enchantment he might never experience again.

A low, pale rectangular shape suddenly emerged from the darkness of the island, shooting out the echoing sound of a speeding motorboat. Two white trails of split water unfurled behind it, and almost instantly the boat was next to him, drowning out the warm tinkling of the piano with the roar of its spray. Dexter lifted himself up on his arms and noticed a figure standing at the steering wheel, two dark eyes watching him across the widening stretch of water—then the boat had passed by and was sweeping in a huge and aimless circle of spray around and around in the center of the lake. Just as randomly, one of the circles straightened out and turned back toward the raft.

"Who's that?" she called out, turning off her motor. She was close enough now that Dexter could make out her swimsuit, which looked like it was made of pink rompers.

The front of the boat struck the raft, and as the raft tilted at a sharp angle, he was thrown toward her. They recognized each other with varying levels of interest.

"Aren't you one of those men we played against this afternoon?" she demanded.

He was.

"Well, do you know how to operate a motorboat? Because if you do, I'd like you to drive this one so I can ride on the surfboard behind it. My name is Judy Jones"—she gave him a ridiculous smirk—or rather, what she attempted to make into a smirk, because no matter how much she twisted her mouth, it wasn't grotesque at all, it was simply beautiful—"and I live in a house over there on the island, and in that house there's a man waiting for me. When he pulled up to the door, I took off from the dock because he tells me I'm his ideal."

A fish leaped from the water while a star sparkled overhead, and the lights surrounding the lake glowed brightly. Dexter sat next to Judy Jones as she described how her boat operated. Moments later, she was in the water, swimming toward the floating surfboard with smooth, flowing strokes. Observing her movement required no effort from the eye, like watching a tree branch sway in the breeze or a seagull soar through the air. Her arms, tanned to a rich butternut shade, moved gracefully through the pale platinum ripples, with her elbow emerging first, then sweeping her forearm back in a rhythm like cascading water, before extending forward and downward, cutting a path through the water ahead.

They headed out onto the lake; when he turned around, Dexter noticed she was kneeling on the back end of the surfboard, which was now tilted upward.

"Go faster," she called, "as fast as it'll go."

Obediently, he pushed the lever forward and white spray shot up at the bow. When he glanced back again, the girl was standing on the rushing board with her arms stretched wide and her eyes raised toward the moon.

"It's terribly cold," she yelled. "What's your name?"

He told her.

"Well, why don't you come to dinner tomorrow night?"

His heart flipped like the boat's flywheel, and once again, her offhand impulse changed the entire course of his life.

Chapter 3

The next evening, as he waited for her to come downstairs, Dexter filled the comfortable, luxurious summer room and the adjoining sun porch with images of the men who had already been in love with Judy Jones. He understood what kind of men they were—the type who had arrived at college from elite preparatory schools, wearing elegant clothing and sporting the deep tans that came from healthy summers spent outdoors. He had recognized that, in certain ways, he was superior to these men. He was fresher and more powerful. However, by admitting to himself that he wanted his future children to resemble them, he was acknowledging that he was merely the raw, sturdy material from which such refined people would always emerge.

When the time came for him to wear fine clothing, he knew who the finest tailors in America were, and the finest tailors in America had crafted the suit he wore that evening. He had developed that distinctive reserve characteristic of his university, which distinguished it from other institutions. He understood the value this particular trait held for him and had embraced it; he realized that being casual in dress and behavior demanded more confidence than being meticulous. But such casualness was meant for his children. His mother's name had been Krimslich. She was a Bohemian from the peasant class and had spoken broken English until the end of her life. Her son had to maintain the established standards.

Shortly after seven o'clock, Judy Jones came downstairs. She was wearing a blue silk afternoon dress, and at first he felt disappointed that she hadn't chosen something more fancy. This disappointment grew stronger when, after they exchanged brief greetings, she walked over to the butler's pantry door and pushed it open to call out: "You can serve dinner, Martha." He had been expecting that a butler would announce dinner and that cocktails would be served first. However, he pushed these thoughts aside as they sat down next to each other on a couch and looked at one another.

"Dad and mom won't be here," she said thoughtfully.

He remembered the last time he had seen her father, and he was relieved that the parents wouldn't be there tonight—they might question who he was. He had been born in Keeble, a Minnesota village fifty miles farther north, and he always claimed Keeble as his hometown instead of Black Bear Village. Small towns were acceptable places to come from as long as they weren't awkwardly visible and overshadowed by trendy lakeside communities.

They discussed his university, which she had visited many times over the past two years, and the nearby city that provided Sherry Island with its customers, where Dexter would go back the next day to his successful laundry business.

During dinner she fell into a brooding sadness that made Dexter feel anxious. Any irritable comment she made in her husky voice troubled him. Whatever brought a smile to her face—whether it was him, a piece of chicken liver, or nothing at all—it bothered him that her smile seemed to have no connection to genuine happiness or even simple pleasure. When the red edges of her mouth turned downward, it looked less like a smile and more like an invitation for a kiss.

Then, after dinner, she guided him out to the dim sun-porch and intentionally shifted the mood.

"Do you mind if I cry a little?" she said.

"I'm afraid I'm boring you," he replied quickly.

"You're not. I like you. But I've just had an awful afternoon. There was a man I cared about, and this afternoon he told me completely out of nowhere that he was broke. He'd never even suggested it before. Does this sound terribly ordinary?"

"Maybe he was scared to tell you."

"Let's say he was," she replied. "He didn't begin properly. You understand, if I had considered him poor—well, I've been crazy about plenty of poor men, and completely planned to marry every one of them. But in this situation, I hadn't viewed him in that light, and my feelings for him weren't powerful enough to withstand the surprise. It's like a woman casually telling her fiancé that she was a widow. He might not mind widows, but——

"Let's start over," she cut herself off abruptly. "Who are you, anyway?"

For a moment Dexter paused. Then:

"I'm nobody," he declared. "My career is mostly about what might happen in the future."

"Are you poor?"

"No," he said honestly, "I'm likely earning more money than anyone my age in the Northwest. I realize that's an arrogant thing to say, but you told me to be straightforward."

There was a pause. Then she smiled and the corners of her mouth turned downward and an almost unnoticeable movement brought her closer to him, gazing up into his eyes. A knot formed in Dexter's throat, and he waited without breathing for what would happen next, confronting the unpredictable mixture that would emerge mysteriously from the meeting of their lips. Then he understood—she shared her passion with him, generously, intensely, with kisses that weren't a pledge but a completion. They stirred in him not craving that demanded satisfaction but abundance that would require even more abundance ... kisses that were like generosity, producing desire by withholding absolutely nothing.

It didn't take him long to realize that he had wanted Judy Jones ever since he was a proud, longing little boy.

Chapter 4

It started that way—and went on, with different levels of intensity, in exactly the same manner right up to the final outcome. Dexter gave up a piece of himself to the most straightforward and unscrupulous person he had ever encountered. Whatever Judy desired, she pursued with the complete force of her appeal. There was no variation in approach, no maneuvering for advantage or calculated planning of results—there was very little intellectual aspect to any of her relationships. She simply made men aware to the greatest extent of her physical beauty. Dexter had no wish to change her. Her flaws were woven together with a fierce vitality that rose above and vindicated them.

When Judy's head rested against his shoulder that first night and she whispered, "I don't know what's wrong with me. Last night I thought I was in love with a man and tonight I think I'm in love with you"—it struck him as something beautiful and romantic to say. It was that exquisite emotional intensity that he felt he could control and possess, at least for the moment. But a week later he found himself forced to see this same trait in a completely different light. She drove him in her roadster to a picnic supper, and after they ate she vanished, taking her roadster with her and another man. Dexter became tremendously upset and could barely manage to be politely civil to the other people there. When she promised him that she hadn't kissed the other man, he knew she was lying—yet he felt grateful that she had bothered to lie to him.

By the time summer ended, he discovered he was just one of about a dozen men who revolved around her. Each of them had once been her favorite above everyone else—roughly half still enjoyed the comfort of occasional romantic rekindlings. Whenever someone seemed ready to give up after being ignored for too long, she would give him a brief, sweet moment that kept him hanging on for another year or more. Judy launched these attacks on the vulnerable and beaten-down men without any ill intent, barely aware that her actions caused any harm.

When a new man arrived in town, everyone else was immediately forgotten—all dates were instantly called off.

The frustrating thing about trying to change the situation was that she controlled everything herself. She wasn't the type of girl who could be "conquered" through action—she was immune to wit, she was immune to charisma; if anyone tried these approaches too forcefully, she would instantly shift the relationship to a purely physical level, and under the spell of her physical beauty, both the powerful and the intelligent ended up playing by her rules instead of their own. She found pleasure only in satisfying her own wants and in directly wielding her personal magnetism. Maybe after experiencing so much young love and so many young admirers, she had learned, as a way of protecting herself, to draw all her sustenance from her own inner resources.

After Dexter's initial excitement came restlessness and dissatisfaction. The overwhelming bliss of losing himself in her acted more like a drug than an energizer. It was lucky for his work during the winter that these moments of bliss happened rarely. Early in their relationship, it had seemed for a time that there was a profound and natural mutual attraction—that first August, for instance—three days of long evenings on her dim veranda, of peculiar pale kisses through the late afternoon, in shaded nooks or behind the sheltering lattices of the garden arbors, of mornings when she was fresh as a dream and almost timid at meeting him in the brightness of the dawning day. There was all the bliss of an engagement about it, intensified by his awareness that there was no engagement. It was during those three days that, for the first time, he had asked her to marry him. She said "maybe some day," she said "kiss me," she said "I'd like to marry you," she said "I love you"—she said—nothing.

The three peaceful days came to an end when a man from New York arrived to stay at her home for half of September. Much to Dexter's torment, gossip suggested they were romantically involved. The visitor was the son of a president from a major trust company. However, after a month had passed, word spread that Judy had grown tired of him. During a dance one evening, she spent the entire night sitting in a motorboat with a local admirer, while the New Yorker frantically searched the club trying to find her. She confided to the local suitor that her visitor had become tedious, and two days afterward he departed. People saw her accompanying him to the train station, and witnesses reported that he appeared quite dejected.

On this note the summer came to an end. Dexter was twenty-four, and he found himself increasingly able to do whatever he wanted. He became a member of two clubs in the city and made his home at one of them. While he wasn't exactly a central figure among the single men at these clubs, he made sure to be present at dances where Judy Jones might show up. He could have participated in social events as much as he desired—he was now an eligible young man who was well-liked by the businessmen downtown. His open devotion to Judy Jones had actually strengthened his social standing. However, he had no interest in climbing the social ladder and looked down on the men who were always available for Thursday or Saturday parties and who served as dinner companions for the younger married couples. He was already considering the idea of heading East to New York. He wanted to bring Judy Jones along with him. No amount of reality about the world she had been raised in could destroy his fantasy about how desirable she was.

Remember this—it's the only way to truly understand what he did for her.

Eighteen months after his first encounter with Judy Jones, he got engaged to someone else. Her name was Irene Scheerer, and her father was among those who had always had faith in Dexter. Irene had light hair and was sweet and decent, though slightly heavy, and she had two other men courting her whom she graciously gave up when Dexter officially proposed to her.

Summer, fall, winter, spring, another summer, another fall—he had devoted so much of his active life to the unchangeable lips of Judy Jones. She had treated him with interest, with encouragement, with spite, with indifference, with scorn. She had subjected him to countless small slights and humiliations that were possible in such a situation—as though seeking revenge for his having cared for her at all. She had called to him and ignored him and called to him again, and he had often responded with resentment and suspicious eyes. She had given him overwhelming joy and unbearable torment of the soul. She had caused him endless inconvenience and considerable trouble. She had insulted him, and she had trampled over him, and she had used his feelings for her against his dedication to his work—for her own amusement. She had done everything to him except criticize him—this she had never done—it seemed to him only because doing so might have tainted the complete indifference she displayed and genuinely felt toward him.

When autumn came and went once more, it dawned on him that he could never have Judy Jones. He had to force this reality into his consciousness, but he finally managed to convince himself of it. He would lie awake at night for hours, wrestling with these thoughts. He reminded himself of all the trouble and heartache she had brought him, listing her obvious flaws as a potential wife. Then he would tell himself that he loved her anyway, and eventually he would drift off to sleep. For an entire week, afraid he might imagine hearing her throaty voice on the phone or picture her eyes looking at him across a lunch table, he threw himself into his work, staying late at the office, and at night he would return to plan out his future years.

After a week had passed, he attended a dance and cut in on her just once. For nearly the first time since they had met, he didn't ask her to sit out with him or tell her how beautiful she was. What hurt him was that she didn't seem to notice these missing gestures—that was everything. He felt no jealousy when he saw there was a new man with her that night. He had grown immune to jealousy long ago.

He remained at the dance until late in the evening. He spent an hour sitting with Irene Scheerer, discussing books and music. His knowledge of both subjects was quite limited. However, he was starting to gain control over his own schedule, and he held a somewhat self-important belief that he—the young and already remarkably successful Dexter Green—ought to be more knowledgeable about these matters.

That happened in October, when he was twenty-five years old. In January, Dexter and Irene got engaged. They planned to announce their engagement in June and get married three months after that.

The Minnesota winter dragged on endlessly, and it was nearly May before the winds turned gentle and the snow finally melted into Black Bear Lake. For the first time in more than a year, Dexter felt a sense of peace. Judy Jones had spent time in Florida, then in Hot Springs, and somewhere along the way she had gotten engaged, and somewhere else she had called it off. Initially, when Dexter had firmly decided to let her go, it saddened him that people continued to connect them and ask about her, but once he started being seated next to Irene Scheerer at dinner parties, people stopped asking him about her—instead, they shared news about her with him. He was no longer considered an expert on her life.

May had finally arrived. Dexter wandered through the streets at night when the darkness felt as heavy and wet as rain, amazed that so quickly, with so little accomplished, so much of his joy had already left him. May from the previous year had been defined by Judy's heartbreaking, inexcusable, yet pardoned chaos—it had been one of those exceptional moments when he believed she had actually begun to love him. That small portion of happiness he had traded for this abundance of satisfaction. He understood that Irene would be nothing more than a backdrop behind him, a hand moving gracefully among shining teacups, a voice calling out to children... passion and beauty had vanished, the enchantment of evenings and the marvel of the changing hours and seasons... delicate lips, curving downward, falling to meet his lips and lifting him into a paradise of eyes.... The feeling ran deep within him. He was too vital and spirited for it to fade easily.

In mid-May, when the weather hung for several days on that delicate threshold leading to the depths of summer, he stopped by Irene's house one evening. Their engagement would be announced within a week—nobody would find it surprising. Tonight they would sit side by side on the sofa at the University Club and watch the dancers for an hour. Going out with her gave him a feeling of stability—she was so solidly popular, so remarkably "wonderful."

He climbed the steps of the brownstone house and walked inside.

"Irene," he called.

Mrs. Scheerer came out of the living room to meet him.

"Dexter," she said, "Irene has gone upstairs with a terrible headache. She wanted to go with you, but I made her go to bed."

"Nothing serious, I——"

"Oh, no. She's going to play golf with you in the morning. You can spare her for just one night, can't you, Dexter?"

Her smile was warm and genuine. She and Dexter had a mutual fondness for each other. In the living room, they chatted briefly before he said goodnight.

Returning to the University Club, where he had his rooms, he paused in the doorway for a moment and observed the dancers. He leaned against the doorframe, acknowledged a man or two with a nod, and yawned.

"Hello, darling."

The familiar voice beside him caught him off guard. Judy Jones had abandoned her companion and made her way across the room to where he stood—Judy Jones, a delicate porcelain figure draped in golden fabric: gold woven into a band around her head, gold gleaming from the pointed tips of her slippers beneath her dress's edge. The soft radiance of her face appeared to bloom as she offered him a smile. A current of warmth and brightness swept through the space. His hands, buried deep in his dinner jacket pockets, clenched involuntarily. A rush of sudden anticipation coursed through him.

"When did you get back?" he asked casually.

"Come here and I'll tell you about it."

She turned around and he walked behind her. She had been gone—the amazing fact that she was back almost brought him to tears. She had walked through magical streets, doing things that felt like stirring music. All the mysterious events, all the new and energizing hopes, had disappeared when she left and had now returned with her.

She turned around in the doorway.

"Do you have a car here? If you don't, I do."

"I have a coupé."

In he came, with a rustle of golden fabric. He slammed the door shut. She had stepped into so many cars just like this—in this way—in that way—her back pressed against the leather seat, just so—her elbow resting against the door—waiting. She would have been corrupted long ago if there had been anything capable of corrupting her—except herself—but this was her own essence flowing out.

With considerable effort, he forced himself to start the car and reverse into the street. This meant nothing, he had to remind himself. She had behaved this way before, and he had moved past her, just as he would have written off a bad debt from his ledgers.

He drove slowly downtown and, pretending to be lost in thought, made his way through the empty streets of the business district, which showed signs of life only where a movie theater was releasing its audience or where sickly or aggressive young men hung around in front of pool halls. The sound of clinking glasses and the smack of hands hitting the bar tops came from the saloons, enclosed spaces of shiny glass and grimy yellow light.

She watched him intently, and the silence felt awkward; yet in this moment of crisis, he couldn't think of any casual words that would break the solemnity of the hour. At a suitable corner, he started weaving his way back toward the University Club.

"Have you missed me?" she asked suddenly.

"Everyone missed you."

He wondered if she knew about Irene Scheerer. She had only been back for a day—her time away had coincided almost exactly with his engagement.

"What a comment!" Judy laughed sadly—without sadness. She looked at him with searching eyes. He became absorbed in the dashboard.

"You're more handsome than you used to be," she said thoughtfully. "Dexter, you have the most unforgettable eyes."

He could have laughed at this, but he didn't. It was the kind of thing people said to college sophomores. Still, it cut deep.

"I'm completely exhausted by everything, darling." She addressed everyone as darling, giving the term of endearment a casual, personal sense of friendship. "I wish you would marry me."

The bluntness of this caught him off guard. He should have told her right then that he was planning to marry someone else, but he couldn't bring himself to say it. It would have been just as easy for him to swear that he had never loved her at all.

"I think we'd get along well," she went on in the same tone, "unless you've probably forgotten about me and fallen in love with someone else."

Her confidence was clearly immense. She had essentially said that she found such a thing impossible to believe, that if it were true he had simply committed a childish mistake—and probably just to show off. She would forgive him, because it wasn't a matter of any importance but rather something to be dismissed easily.

"Of course you could never love anybody but me," she went on, "I like the way you love me. Oh, Dexter, have you forgotten last year?"

"No, I haven't forgotten."

"Neither have I!"

Was she genuinely moved—or was she simply swept up by the momentum of her own performance?

"I wish we could be like that again," she said, and he made himself respond:

"I don't think we can."

"I suppose not.... I hear you're pursuing Irene Scheerer quite aggressively."

There wasn't the slightest emphasis on the name, yet Dexter suddenly felt ashamed.

"Oh, take me home," Judy suddenly cried out; "I don't want to go back to that ridiculous dance—with those kids."

Then, as he turned onto the street leading to the residential area, Judy started crying softly to herself. He had never witnessed her cry before.

The dark street grew brighter, and the homes of the wealthy rose up around them. He brought his car to a stop in front of the massive white structure of the Mortimer Jones house, which stood sleepy, magnificent, and bathed in the glory of the wet moonlight. Its solid presence surprised him. The thick walls, the steel beams, and all its width and grandeur existed only to highlight the contrast with the young woman's beauty beside him. The house's strength seemed designed to emphasize her delicate frame—as if to demonstrate what kind of gentle wind a butterfly's wing could create.

He sat completely still, his nerves screaming wildly, terrified that any movement would lead to him pulling her irresistibly into his arms. Two tears had streamed down her damp face and quivered on her upper lip.

"I'm more beautiful than anyone else," she said with a broken voice, "so why can't I find happiness?" Her tearful eyes shattered his composure—her lips curved slowly downward with heartbreaking sorrow: "I want to marry you if you'll accept me, Dexter. You probably think I'm not worth it, but I'll be so beautiful for you, Dexter."

A million expressions of anger, pride, passion, hatred, and tenderness battled for voice on his lips. Then a complete wave of emotion swept over him, washing away the residue of wisdom, convention, doubt, and honor. This was his girl speaking, his own, his beautiful one, his pride.

"Won't you come in?" He heard her take a sharp breath. Waiting.

"All right," his voice was shaking, "I'll come in."

Chapter 5

It was odd that he never regretted that night, not when it ended or even years later. When he looked back after ten years had passed, the fact that Judy's passion for him lasted only a month didn't seem important at all. It also didn't matter that by giving in to her, he caused himself much deeper pain eventually and seriously hurt Irene Scheerer along with Irene's parents, who had been kind to him. There wasn't anything vivid enough about Irene's sorrow to leave a lasting impression on his memory.

Dexter was fundamentally tough-minded. What the city thought about his actions didn't matter to him at all, not because he planned to leave town, but because any outside opinions about the situation struck him as shallow. He was completely unmoved by what people thought. And when he realized it was hopeless, that he didn't have the ability to truly change or keep Judy Jones, he held no grudge against her. He loved her, and he would continue loving her until he became too old to love—but he couldn't have her. So he experienced the profound pain that only the strong can endure, just as he had briefly experienced profound happiness.

Even the complete falseness of Judy's reasons for ending their engagement—claiming she didn't want to "take him away" from Irene when that was exactly what she had wanted all along—didn't disgust him. He was past feeling any disgust or finding any humor in it.

He traveled East in February planning to sell his laundries and make his home in New York—but when war reached America in March, everything changed. He went back West, turned the business over to his partner, and enrolled in the first officers' training camp in late April. He was among the thousands of young men who welcomed the war with some sense of relief, grateful for freedom from complicated emotional entanglements.

––––––––––––––––

Chapter 6

This story isn't his biography, remember, even though details slip in that have nothing to do with the dreams he had as a young man. We're almost finished with those dreams and with him now. There's just one more incident to tell here, and it takes place seven years later.

It happened in New York, where he had achieved great success—such remarkable success that no obstacle seemed insurmountable to him. He was thirty-two years old, and apart from one brief trip right after the war ended, he hadn't traveled west in seven years. A man called Devlin from Detroit visited his office on business matters, and it was then and there that this event took place, effectively bringing this particular chapter of his life to a close.

"So you're from the Midwest," said the man Devlin with casual curiosity. "That's interesting—I thought guys like you were probably born and raised on Wall Street. You know—the wife of one of my best friends in Detroit came from your city. I was an usher at the wedding."

Dexter waited without any sense of dread about what was approaching.

"Judy Simms," Devlin said without much interest. "She used to be Judy Jones."

"Yes, I knew her." A weary irritation washed over him. He had heard, naturally, that she had gotten married— maybe on purpose he had chosen not to learn anything more.

"Really nice girl," Devlin mused without much thought, "I feel kind of sorry for her."

"Why?" Something inside Dexter became instantly alert and receptive.

"Oh, Lud Simms has really fallen apart in some ways. I don't mean he mistreats her, but he drinks heavily and runs around with other women———"

"Doesn't she run around?"

"No. She stays at home with her kids."

"Oh."

"She's a little too old for him," said Devlin.

"Too old!" Dexter exclaimed. "What are you talking about? She's only twenty-seven."

He was consumed by a crazy idea of running out into the streets and catching a train to Detroit. He jumped to his feet suddenly.

"I guess you're busy," Devlin said apologetically. "I didn't realize———"

"No, I'm not busy," Dexter said, trying to keep his voice steady. "I'm not busy at all. Not busy at all. Did you say she was twenty-seven? No, I said she was twenty-seven."

"Yes, you did," Devlin agreed with a dry tone.

"Go on, then. Go on."

"What do you mean?"

"About Judy Jones."

Devlin looked at him helplessly.

"Well, that's it—I've told you everything there is to know. He treats her terribly. Oh, they're not going to divorce or anything like that. When he's especially awful to her, she forgives him. Actually, I think she loves him. She was beautiful when she first arrived in Detroit."

A beautiful girl! The phrase seemed completely ridiculous to Dexter.

"Isn't she a pretty girl anymore?"

"Oh, she's all right."

"Listen," said Dexter, dropping into his seat abruptly, "I'm confused. You're telling me she was a 'pretty girl' and then you say she's 'all right.' I don't get what you're trying to say—Judy Jones wasn't just a pretty girl, not at all. She was absolutely stunning. I mean, I knew her, I really knew her. She was——"

Devlin laughed pleasantly.

"I'm not trying to pick a fight," he said. "I think Judy's a nice girl and I like her. I can't figure out how a guy like Lud Simms could fall head over heels for her, but he did." Then he added: "Most women like her."

Dexter studied Devlin carefully, his mind racing with the thought that there had to be an explanation for this behavior—perhaps some lack of awareness on the man's part, or maybe some personal grudge.

"Many women lose their beauty just like that," Devlin said, snapping his fingers. "You must have witnessed it yourself. Maybe I've forgotten how beautiful she looked on her wedding day. I've seen her so often since then, you understand. She does have lovely eyes."

A kind of numbness came over Dexter. For the first time in his life he wanted to get completely drunk. He realized he was laughing too loudly at something Devlin had said, but he couldn't remember what it was or why it seemed amusing. When Devlin left a few minutes later, he stretched out on his couch and gazed through the window at the New York skyline, where the sun was setting in muted, beautiful tones of pink and gold.

He had believed that with nothing left to lose, he was finally untouchable—but he realized he had just lost something even more precious, as certainly as if he had married Judy Jones and watched her slip away right in front of him.

The dream had vanished. Something had been stolen from him. In a kind of desperation, he pressed his palms against his eyes and struggled to conjure an image of the waves washing against Sherry Island's shore and the moonlit porch, and the gingham fabric on the golf course and the harsh sun and the golden hue of the soft hair on her neck. And her lips moist from his kisses and her eyes sorrowful with sadness and her vitality like crisp new linen in the morning. But these things no longer existed in the world! They had been real and now they were gone forever.

For the first time in years, tears were flowing down his face. But now they were for himself. He didn't care about lips and eyes and gestures. He wanted to feel something, but he couldn't make himself care. He had left that place behind and could never return. The doors had shut, the sun had set, and there was no beauty except the cold beauty of steel that endures forever. Even the sorrow he might have been able to bear had been left behind in that land of dreams, of youth, of life's abundance, where his winter fantasies had once thrived.

"A long time ago," he said, "a long time ago, there was something inside me, but now that something is gone. Now that something is gone, that something is gone. I can't cry. I can't care. That something will never come back."

The Baby Party

When John Andros felt his age weighing on him, he found comfort in knowing that life would go on through his child. The dark horns of death seemed quieter when he heard his child's footsteps or listened to his child's voice chattering nonsensical phrases to him over the phone. This phone call happened every afternoon at three o'clock when his wife rang the office from their country home, and he began to anticipate it as one of the brightest moments of his day.

He wasn't physically old, but his life had been one struggle after another, like climbing a series of steep, rocky hills. Now at thirty-eight, having fought and won his battles against poor health and financial hardship, he held fewer illusions than most people his age. Even his feelings toward his young daughter were complicated. She had disrupted the passionate romance he shared with his wife, and she was the reason they now lived in a suburban town, where they traded city conveniences for fresh country air, only to deal with constant problems finding and keeping household help and the exhausting daily routine of commuter train travel.

It was little Ede as a clear example of youth that mainly fascinated him. He enjoyed holding her on his lap and closely studying her sweet-smelling, soft scalp and her eyes with their morning-blue irises. After paying this tribute, John was satisfied to let the nurse take her away. After ten minutes, the child's sheer energy annoyed him; he tended to get angry when things got broken, and one Sunday afternoon when she had ruined a bridge game by permanently hiding the ace of spades, he had caused such a commotion that it made his wife cry.

This was ridiculous and John felt embarrassed about his reaction. It was bound to happen that such changes would occur, and it was unrealistic to expect little Ede to spend all her time indoors in the upstairs nursery when she was growing into what her mother described as more of a "real person" each day.

She was two and a half years old, and this afternoon she was attending a baby party. Her mother, grown-up Edith, had called the office to share this information, and little Ede had confirmed the plans by yelling "I yam going to a pantry!" directly into John's unsuspecting left ear.

"Stop by the Markeys' place when you get home, will you, sweetheart?" her mother continued. "It's going to be amusing. Ede's planning to be all dressed up in her new pink dress——"

The conversation ended suddenly with a harsh squawk that showed the telephone had been yanked forcefully to the floor. John chuckled and made up his mind to catch an early train out of town; the idea of attending a baby party at someone else's home entertained him.

"What a perfect disaster!" he thought with amusement. "A dozen mothers, and every single one focused only on her own child. All the babies destroying things and reaching for the cake, and each mother going home convinced of her own child's quiet superiority over all the other children there."

He was in a good mood today—everything in his life was going better than it ever had before. When he stepped off the train at his station, he shook his head at a persistent taxi driver and started walking up the long hill toward his house through the crisp December twilight. It was only six o'clock, but the moon was already visible, shining with magnificent brightness on the thin, powdery snow that covered the lawns.

As he strolled along, filling his lungs with the crisp air, his joy grew stronger, and the thought of attending a children's party became increasingly appealing to him. He started to think about how Ede measured up against other kids her age, and whether the pink dress she would be wearing was perhaps too sophisticated and grown-up for her. Picking up his pace, he spotted his own home, where the lights from an old Christmas tree were still twinkling in the window, but he walked past his driveway. The celebration was taking place at the Markeys' house right next door.

As he climbed the brick step and pressed the doorbell, he noticed voices coming from inside the house, relieved that he hadn't arrived too late. He lifted his head to listen more carefully—these weren't children's voices, but they were loud and shrill with anger. There were at least three different voices, and one of them, which escalated into a hysterical sob as he stood there listening, he instantly recognized as his wife's.

"There's been some trouble," he thought quickly.

Trying the door, he discovered it was unlocked and pushed it open.

The baby party started at four-thirty, but Edith Andros, cleverly figuring that the new dress would make a more dramatic impression against clothes that were already wrinkled, decided that she and little Ede would arrive at five. When they showed up, the party was already in full swing. Four baby girls and nine baby boys, each one with their hair curled and bodies washed and dressed with all the attention of a proud and protective heart, were dancing to music from a phonograph. No more than two or three were ever dancing at the same time, but since all of them were constantly moving around, running back and forth to their mothers for support, the overall impression was the same.

As Edith and her daughter walked in, the music was momentarily overwhelmed by a continuous chorus of voices, mostly repeating the word "cute" and aimed at little Ede, who stood there looking shyly around while nervously touching the hem of her pink dress. She wasn't kissed—this was the era of hygiene consciousness—but she was guided along a line of mothers, each one cooing "cu-u-ute" at her and gently holding her small pink hand before passing her along to the next woman. With some gentle encouragement and a few light nudges, she was drawn into the dancing and became an enthusiastic participant in the party.

Edith stood by the door chatting with Mrs. Markey while keeping watch over the small figure in the pink dress. She didn't like Mrs. Markey much; she thought her both snobbish and ordinary, but since John and Joe Markey got along well and rode the commuter train together every morning, the two women maintained an elaborate act of close friendship. They constantly scolded each other for "never visiting," and they were always making plans for get-togethers that started with "We really must have you over for dinner soon, and then we can catch a show," but these plans never went anywhere.

"Little Ede looks absolutely adorable," said Mrs. Markey, smiling and wetting her lips in a manner that Edith found especially disgusting. "So mature—I can't believe it!"

Edith wondered if "little Ede" was a reference to the fact that Billy Markey, despite being several months younger, weighed nearly five pounds more. Taking a cup of tea, she settled onto a sofa with two other women and dove into the real purpose of the afternoon, which naturally involved sharing her child's latest achievements and charming misbehaviors.

An hour went by. The children grew tired of dancing and turned to more energetic activities. They ran into the dining room, circled around the large table, and attempted to reach the kitchen door, where a rescue team of mothers intercepted them. After being gathered up, they immediately escaped again, rushing back to the dining room to try the familiar swinging door once more. Parents began using the word "overheated," and small perspiring foreheads were wiped with small white handkerchiefs. A collective effort to get the babies to sit down commenced, but the children wriggled off their parents' laps with demanding shouts of "Down! Down!" and the mad dash into the captivating dining room started all over again.

This part of the party ended when the refreshments arrived, featuring a large cake with two candles and small plates of vanilla ice cream. Billy Markey, a chubby, cheerful baby with red hair and slightly curved legs, blew out the candles and pressed his thumb experimentally into the white frosting. The refreshments were handed out, and the children ate eagerly but in an orderly fashion—they had been exceptionally well-behaved throughout the entire afternoon. These were contemporary babies who ate and slept on consistent schedules, which meant they had pleasant temperaments and healthy, rosy faces—such a calm gathering wouldn't have been achievable three decades earlier.

After the refreshments, people gradually started leaving. Edith looked nervously at her watch—it was nearly six o'clock, and John still hadn't shown up. She wanted him to see Ede with the other children—to see how well-mannered and courteous and bright she was, and how the only ice-cream stain on her dress was from some that had fallen from her chin when someone bumped into her from behind.

"You're a sweetheart," she whispered to her child, pulling her close against her knee. "Do you know you're a sweetheart? Do you know you're a sweetheart?"

Ede laughed. "Bow-wow," she said suddenly.

"Bow-wow?" Edith looked around. "There isn't any bow-wow."

"Bow-wow," Ede said again. "I want a bow-wow."

Edith followed the small pointing finger.

"That's not a dog, sweetheart, that's a teddy bear."

"Bear?"

"Yes, that's a teddy bear, and it belongs to Billy Markey. You don't want Billy Markey's teddy bear, do you?"

Ede did want it.

She pulled away from her mother and walked over to Billy Markey, who was clutching the toy tightly against his chest. Ede stood there looking at him with unreadable eyes, and Billy laughed.

Edith, now an adult, glanced at her watch once more, this time with growing impatience.

The party had gradually emptied out until only two babies were left, along with Ede and Billy—and one of those two was only still there because he had managed to hide himself underneath the dining room table. John's absence was really selfish of him. It demonstrated such a lack of pride in his child. Several other fathers had shown up, at least half a dozen of them, to pick up their wives, and they had lingered for a bit to watch what was happening.

There was a sudden cry. Ede had grabbed Billy's teddy bear by yanking it forcefully from his arms, and when Billy

44

tried to get it back, she had carelessly shoved him to the ground.

"Why, Ede!" her mother exclaimed, holding back the urge to laugh.

Joe Markey, an attractive, broad-shouldered thirty-five-year-old man, lifted his son and helped him stand up. "You're quite something," he said cheerfully. "Letting a girl knock you down! You're really something."

"Did he bump his head?" Mrs. Markey asked anxiously as she returned from escorting the second-to-last remaining mother to the door.

"No-o-o-o," Markey cried out. "He hit something different, didn't you, Billy? He hit something different."

Billy had completely forgotten about the bump and was already trying to get his property back. He grabbed one of the bear's legs that was sticking out from Ede's encircling arms and pulled on it, but he couldn't manage to free it.

"No," Ede said firmly.

Suddenly, encouraged by the success of her earlier half-accidental move, Ede dropped the teddy bear, placed her hands on Billy's shoulders and pushed him backward off his feet.

This time his landing was far from gentle; his head struck the bare floor just beyond the edge of the rug with a dull, hollow thud, and he immediately gasped and let out a cry of pain.

Instantly, the room erupted into chaos. Markey cried out and rushed toward his son, but his wife reached the hurt child first and swept him up into her arms.

"Oh, Billy," she exclaimed, "what a horrible bump! She should be spanked."

Edith, who had hurried straight to her daughter, overheard this comment, and her lips pressed tightly together.

"Why, Ede," she whispered without much feeling, "you naughty girl!"

Ede suddenly threw her little head back and burst into laughter. It was a loud laugh, a triumphant laugh filled with victory and challenge and scorn. Unfortunately, it was also a contagious laugh. Before her mother understood how delicate the situation was, she had also laughed, a clear, unmistakable laugh much like the baby's, carrying the same undertones.

Then, just as suddenly, she stopped.

Mrs. Markey's face had turned red with rage, and Markey, who had been gently touching the back of the baby's head with his finger, glanced at her with a frown.

"It's already swollen," he said with a hint of disapproval in his voice. "I'll get some witch hazel."

But Mrs. Markey had lost her temper. "I don't see anything funny about a child being hurt!" she said with a shaking voice.

Little Ede had been watching her mother with curiosity during this time. She observed that her own laughter had triggered her mother's laughter, and she found herself wondering whether the same cause would consistently produce the same result. With this in mind, she decided this was the perfect moment to tilt her head back and laugh once more.

To her mother, the extra laughter was the last straw that made the whole situation feel completely out of control. She pressed her handkerchief against her mouth and couldn't stop giggling. This was more than just nerves—she had the strange feeling that she was laughing alongside her child—they were sharing this moment of laughter together.

It was, in a sense, an act of rebellion—the two of them standing against everyone else.

While Markey hurried upstairs to the bathroom to get ointment, his wife paced back and forth, rocking the screaming boy in her arms.

"Please go home!" she suddenly burst out. "The child is badly injured, and if you don't have the decency to be quiet, you'd better go home."

"Very well," said Edith, her own temper rising. "I've never seen anyone make such a mountain out of——"

"Get out!" Mrs. Markey shouted frantically. "There's the door, get out—I never want to see you in our house again. You or your kid either!"

Edith had grabbed her daughter's hand and was hurrying toward the door, but when she heard this comment she stopped and spun around, her face twisting with anger.

"Don't you dare call her that!"

Mrs. Markey didn't respond but kept pacing back and forth, mumbling to herself and to Billy in a voice too quiet to hear.

Edith began to cry.

"I'm leaving!" she cried through her tears. "I've never encountered anyone so rude and vulgar in my entire life. I'm actually glad your baby got knocked down—he's just a chubby little idiot anyway."

Joe Markey reached the bottom of the stairs just in time to hear this comment.

"Why, Mrs. Andros," he said sharply, "can't you see the child is injured? You really need to get a grip on yourself."

"Control myself!" Edith burst out, her voice breaking. "You'd better ask her to control herself. I've never heard anyone so vulgar in my entire life."

"She's insulting me!" Mrs. Markey was now furious with anger. "Did you hear what she said, Joe? I want you to throw her out. If she refuses to leave, just grab her by the shoulders and force her out!"

"Don't you dare touch me!" Edith shouted. "I'm leaving as fast as I can find my coat!"

Blinded by tears, she took a step toward the hall. At that exact moment, the door opened and John Andros walked in with a worried expression.

"John!" Edith cried out, and ran to him frantically.

"What's wrong? Why, what's wrong?"

"They're—they're throwing me out!" she cried, falling against him. "He had just started to grab me by the shoulders and throw me out. I want my coat!"

"That's not true," Markey protested quickly. "No one's going to kick you out." He looked at John. "No one's going to kick her out," he said again. "She's———"

"What do you mean 'put her out'?" John demanded suddenly. "What's all this talk about, anyway?"

"Oh, let's go!" Edith exclaimed. "I want to go. They're so ordinary, John!"

"Look here!" Markey's face darkened. "You've said that enough times. You're acting kind of crazy."

"They called Ede a brat!"

For the second time that afternoon, little Ede showed her feelings at exactly the wrong moment. Bewildered and scared by the raised voices around her, she started to cry, and her tears made it clear that she had taken the insult deeply to heart.

"What's the point of this?" John burst out. "Are you insulting your guests in your own home?"

"It seems to me it's your wife that's done the insulting!" answered Markey crisply. "In fact, your baby there started all the trouble."

John let out a scornful snort. "Are you calling a little baby names?" he asked. "That's really manly behavior!"

"Don't talk to him, John," Edith insisted. "Find my coat!"

"You must be in a really bad state," John continued angrily, "if you have to take your anger out on a defenseless little baby."

"I've never heard anything so damn twisted in my life," Markey shouted. "If that wife of yours would just shut her mouth for a minute——"

"Hold on! You're not speaking to a woman and child right now——"

There was a brief interruption. Edith had been searching around on a chair for her coat, and Mrs. Markey had been staring at her with fierce, furious eyes. All at once she placed Billy down on the couch, where he instantly quit crying and pulled himself up to sit, and walking into the hallway she swiftly located Edith's coat and gave it to her without saying anything. Then she returned to the couch, lifted Billy up, and cradling him in her arms gazed once more at Edith with fierce, furious eyes. The interruption had lasted less than thirty seconds.

"Your wife walks in here and starts yelling about how ordinary we are!" Markey exploded angrily. "Well, if we're so damn ordinary, you should stay away! And what's more, you better leave right now!"

Again John let out a brief, scornful laugh.

"You're not just ordinary," he shot back, "you're clearly a terrible bully—especially when there are defenseless women and children nearby." He reached for the doorknob and pulled the door open. "Come on, Edith."

Taking her daughter in her arms, his wife walked outside, and John, still glaring at Markey with contempt, began to follow her.

"Hold on!" Markey stepped forward; he was shaking slightly, and two prominent veins on his temple suddenly filled with blood. "You don't think you can get away with that, do you? Not with me?"

Without saying anything, John walked out the door and left it open.

Edith, tears still streaming down her face, had begun walking home. John watched her until she reached her own walkway, then turned back toward the illuminated doorway where Markey was carefully making his way down the slick steps. He removed his overcoat and hat, throwing them off the path into the snow. Then, slipping slightly on the frozen walkway, he moved forward.

At the first hit, both of them lost their footing and crashed hard onto the sidewalk, managing to get halfway up before dragging each other back down again. They managed to get better traction in the light snow beside the walkway and charged at each other, both throwing wild punches while trampling the snow into a slushy mess beneath their feet.

The street was empty, and apart from their brief exhausted breaths and the muffled noise when one or the other stumbled into the wet, muddy slush, they battled without speaking, each clearly visible to the other in the bright moonlight as well as in the golden light streaming from the open doorway. Multiple times they both fell down at the same time, and then for a period the fight continued frantically across the grass.

For ten, fifteen, twenty minutes they battled there mindlessly in the moonlight. They had both removed their coats and vests at some quietly agreed-upon moment, and now their shirts hung from their backs in soaked, pulpy tatters. Both were ripped and bleeding and so drained that they could remain upright only when their positioning allowed them to lean on each other—the force, the simple exertion of a strike, would knock them both down to their hands and knees.

But exhaustion wasn't what brought the fight to an end, and the complete pointlessness of their struggle was actually a reason to keep going. They stopped because while they were wrestling on the ground, locked together, they heard a man's footsteps approaching along the sidewalk. They had somehow rolled into the shadows, and when those footsteps reached their ears, they immediately stopped fighting, stopped moving, stopped breathing, lying pressed together like two children playing a game of cowboys and Indians until the footsteps faded away. Then, stumbling back to their feet, they stared at each other like two drunk men.

"I'll be damned if I'm going on with this thing any more," Markey declared, his voice thick with emotion.

"I'm not continuing with this anymore either," said John Andros. "I've had enough of this whole situation."

Again they looked at each other, this time with sullen expressions, as if each one suspected the other of pushing him toward another round of fighting. Markey spat out a mouthful of blood from his cut lip; then he swore quietly, and picking up his coat and vest, he shook the snow off them with a surprised manner, as if how wet they had gotten was his only concern in the world.

"Want to come in and wash up?" he asked suddenly.

"No, thanks," said John. "I should be heading home—my wife will be worried."

He also grabbed his coat and vest, followed by his overcoat and hat. Drenched and dripping with sweat, it felt ridiculous that he had been wearing all these layers less than thirty minutes earlier.

"Well—good night," he said hesitantly.

Suddenly they both walked toward each other and shook hands. This wasn't just a casual handshake: John Andros put his arm around Markey's shoulder and gently patted him on the back for a moment.

"No harm done," he said in a broken voice.

"No—you?"

"No, no harm done."

"Well," said John Andros after a moment, "I think I'll say good night."

"Good night."

Limping slightly and carrying his clothes over his arm, John Andros turned and walked away. The moonlight remained bright as he left the dark area of trampled earth and crossed the lawn between. Down at the station, half a mile in the distance, he could hear the rumbling sound of the seven o'clock train.

"But you must have been out of your mind," Edith exclaimed, her voice breaking. "I thought you were going to work everything out and make peace with each other. That's the reason I left."

"Did you want us to fix it up?" "Of course not, I never want to see them again. But I thought that was obviously what you were planning to do." She was gently applying iodine to the bruises on his neck and back while he sat calmly in a hot bath. "I'm going to call the doctor," she said firmly. "You might have internal injuries."

He shook his head. "Not a chance," he replied. "I don't want this spreading all around town."

"I still don't understand how it all happened."

"Neither do I." He smiled grimly. "I suppose these baby parties are pretty tough events."

"Well, one thing—" Edith suggested hopefully, "I'm certainly glad we have steak in the house for tomorrow's dinner."

"Why?"

"For your eye, of course. Do you know I almost ordered veal? Wasn't that the luckiest thing?"

Half an hour later, dressed except for the fact that his neck couldn't fit into any collar, John moved his arms and legs experimentally in front of the mirror. "I think I'll get myself in better shape," he said thoughtfully. "I must be getting old."

"You mean so that next time you can beat him?"

"I did beat him," he declared. "At least, I gave him as good as I got. And there won't be a next time. Don't go around calling people common anymore. If you run into any trouble, just grab your coat and head home. Do you understand?"

"Yes, dear," she said quietly. "I was really foolish and now I get it."

Out in the hallway, he stopped suddenly at the baby's door.

"Is she asleep?"

"Fast asleep. But you can go in and take a look at her— just to say good night."

They quietly entered the room and leaned over the bed together. Little Ede, with rosy cheeks glowing with health and her small pink hands clasped tightly together, was sleeping peacefully in the cool, dim room. John reached across the bed's railing and gently brushed his hand over her silky hair.

"She's asleep," he whispered in confusion.

"Of course, after spending an afternoon like that."

"Mrs. Andros," the Black maid's hushed voice carried in from the hallway, "Mr. and Mrs. Markey are downstairs and want to see you. Mr. Markey is all beaten up, ma'am. His face looks like raw meat. And Mrs. Markey appears very angry."

"What incredible nerve!" Edith exclaimed. "Just tell them we're not home. I wouldn't go downstairs for anything in the world."

"You most certainly will." John's voice was hard and set.

"What?"

"You're going downstairs right now, and on top of that, no matter what that other woman does, you're going to apologize for what you said this afternoon. After that, you never have to see her again."

"Why—John, I can't."

"You have to. And just remember that she probably hated coming over here twice as much as you hate going downstairs."

"Aren't you coming? Do I have to go alone?" "I'll be down—in just a minute."

John Andros waited until she had shut the door behind her; then he leaned over to the bed, and lifting his daughter along with all her blankets, settled into the rocking chair while holding her close in his arms. She stirred slightly, and he caught his breath, but she was deep in sleep, and within moments she was lying peacefully in the curve of his elbow. Gradually he lowered his head until his cheek touched her golden hair. "Sweet little girl," he whispered softly. "Sweet little girl, sweet little girl."

John Andros finally understood what he had fought for so fiercely that evening. He had it now, he owned it forever, and for some time he sat there swaying very slowly back and forth in the darkness.

———————————

Forgiveness

Chapter 1

There was once a priest with cold, watery eyes who wept cold tears in the quiet of the night. He cried because the afternoons stretched long and warm, and he couldn't achieve complete spiritual union with our Lord. Sometimes, around four o'clock, Swedish girls would rustle along the path outside his window, and their sharp laughter created a harsh discord that made him pray out loud for evening to arrive. When twilight came, the laughter and voices grew softer, but several times he had walked past Romberg's Drug Store at dusk when the yellow lights glowed inside and the nickel soda fountain taps gleamed, and he had found the scent of inexpensive soap hanging desperately sweet in the air. He took that route when returning from hearing confessions on Saturday nights, and he became careful to walk on the opposite side of the street so the soap's fragrance would drift upward before reaching his nose as it floated, much like incense, toward the summer moon.

But there was no way to escape the blazing insanity of four o'clock. From his window, stretching as far as his eyes could reach, Dakota wheat crowded the Red River valley. The wheat was horrifying to behold, and the carpet design that he stared at in anguish made his mind wander through bizarre mazes, always exposed to the relentless sun.

One afternoon when his mind had grown as sluggish as an old clock winding down, his housekeeper brought a beautiful, intense eleven-year-old boy named Rudolph Miller into his study. The little boy settled into a spot where sunlight streamed in, while the priest sat at his walnut desk and pretended to be deeply occupied with work. He was trying to hide his relief that someone had finally entered his troubled room.

He soon turned around and discovered himself looking directly into two huge, piercing eyes that sparkled with brilliant flashes of deep blue light. For an instant their look shocked him—then he realized that his visitor was completely terrified.

"Your mouth is trembling," said Father Schwartz, in a worn and exhausted voice.

The little boy covered his trembling mouth with his hand.

"Are you in trouble?" Father Schwartz asked sharply. "Take your hand away from your mouth and tell me what's wrong."

The boy—Father Schwartz now recognized him as the son of a parishioner, Mr. Miller, who worked as a freight agent—reluctantly moved his hand away from his mouth and began to speak in a desperate whisper.

"Father Schwartz—I've committed a terrible sin."

"A sin against purity?"

"No, Father ... worse."

Father Schwartz's body jerked sharply.

"Have you killed somebody?"

"No—but I'm afraid—" the voice rose to a shrill whimper.

"Do you want to go to confession?"

The little boy shook his head sadly. Father Schwartz cleared his throat so he could soften his voice and say something gentle and compassionate. In this moment, he needed to set aside his own pain and try to act with divine grace. He silently repeated a prayer, hoping that God would guide him to respond properly.

"Tell me what you've done," said his new soft voice.

The little boy gazed at him through his tears and felt comforted by the sense of inner strength that the troubled priest conveyed. Giving himself over to this man as completely as he could manage, Rudolph Miller started to share his story.

"Last Saturday, three days ago, my father told me I had to go to confession because I hadn't been in a month, while the rest of the family goes every week, and I had been skipping. I was fine with going, I didn't really mind. I kept putting it off until after dinner because I was playing with a group of kids, and when father asked me if I had gone, I told him 'no,' so he grabbed me by the neck and said 'You go now,' and I said 'All right,' so I walked over to the church. He shouted after me: 'Don't come back until you go.'..."

Chapter 2

"On Saturday, Three Days Ago."

The soft curtain of the confessional shifted its gloomy folds, revealing only the bottom of an elderly man's worn shoe. Behind the curtain an eternal soul was alone with God and Reverend Adolphus Schwartz, the parish priest. Sound emerged, a strained whisper, hissing and quiet, interrupted occasionally by the priest's voice asking audible questions.

Rudolph Miller knelt in the church pew next to the confessional booth and waited, tensely trying both to listen and not to listen to what was happening inside. The fact that he could hear the priest's voice worried him. He would be next, and the three or four other people waiting might eavesdrop without shame while he confessed his breaking of the Sixth and Ninth Commandments.

Rudolph had never cheated on his wife or even desired his neighbor's spouse—but admitting to the related sins was especially difficult to think about. By contrast, he found some comfort in his less embarrassing moral failures—they created a dull backdrop that made the dark stain of sexual wrongdoing on his soul stand out even more.

He had been covering his ears with his hands, hoping that his refusal to listen would be noticed, and that someone would show him the same consideration in return, when a sudden movement of the person confessing made him quickly bury his face in the bend of his elbow. Fear took on a physical presence, forcing itself into the space between his heart and his lungs. He had to try with everything he had to feel genuine remorse for his sins—not because he was scared, but because he had wronged God. He needed to convince God that he was truly sorry, and to do that he first had to convince himself. After an intense emotional battle, he managed to work up a shaky sense of self-pity, and decided he was finally ready. If he could keep all other thoughts out of his mind and maintain this emotional state intact until he entered that large upright coffin, he would have made it through another test of his faith.

For a while, though, a devilish idea had started to take hold of him. He could head home right now, before his turn arrived, and tell his mother that he had gotten there too late and discovered the priest had already left. This option, unfortunately, carried the danger of getting caught in a lie. As another choice, he could claim that he had gone to confession, but this would mean he'd have to skip communion the next day, because taking communion with an unclean soul would become poison in his mouth, and he would collapse weak and condemned at the altar rail.

Again Father Schwartz's voice became audible.

"And for your——"

The words became an indistinct, rough murmur, and Rudolph jumped up excitedly. He realized it would be impossible for him to go to confession that afternoon. He paused, filled with nervous tension. Then sounds emerged from the confessional—a tap, a creak, and a prolonged rustling. The partition had dropped and the velvet curtain shook. Temptation had arrived too late for him....

"Bless me, Father, for I have sinned.... I confess to Almighty God and to you, Father, that I have sinned.... Since my last confession it has been one month and three days.... I accuse myself of—taking the Name of the Lord in vain...."

This was a simple transgression. His profanity had been nothing more than false bravado—recounting it was barely different from boasting.

"... of being mean to an old lady."

The pale shadow shifted slightly on the crossed wooden slat.

"How, my child?"

"Old Mrs. Swenson," Rudolph's whisper rose with excitement. "She took our baseball after we accidentally hit it through her window, and she refused to give it back, so we spent the whole afternoon shouting 'Twenty-three, Skidoo' at her. Then around five o'clock she had some kind of episode, and they had to call the doctor."

"Go on, my child."

"Of—of not believing I was my parents' son."

"What?" The question came out clearly startled.

"Of not believing that I was the son of my parents."

"Why not?"

"Oh, just pride," the penitent replied casually.

"You mean you thought you were too good to be the son of your parents?"

"Yes, Father." His tone was noticeably less enthusiastic now.

"Go on."

"Of being disobedient and calling my mother names. Of talking badly about people behind their backs. Of smoking——"

Rudolph had now gone through all the minor wrongdoings and was getting closer to the sins that caused him terrible pain to confess. He pressed his fingers against his face like prison bars, as though trying to squeeze out the shame that filled his heart.

"Of dirty words and inappropriate thoughts and desires," he whispered very quietly.

"How often?"

"I don't know."

"Once a week? Twice a week?"

"Twice a week."

"Did you give in to these desires?"

"No, Father."

"Were you alone when you had them?"

"No, Father. I was with two boys and a girl."

"Don't you understand, my child, that you need to stay away from situations that lead to sin, not just avoid the sin itself? Bad company leads to bad desires, and bad desires lead to bad actions. Where were you when this took place?"

"In a barn behind——"

"I don't want to hear any names," the priest interrupted sharply.

"Well, it was up in the barn's loft where this girl and a guy were talking—saying inappropriate things, and I stayed to listen."

"You should have left—you should have told the girl to leave."

He should have left! He couldn't explain to Father Schwartz how his heart had raced, how an unusual, thrilling excitement had taken hold of him when those strange things had been spoken. Maybe in those places where troubled youth gather, among the emotionally hardened and defiant girls, one might discover those who have experienced the most intense passion.

"Do you have anything else to tell me?"

"I don't think so, Father."

Rudolph felt an enormous sense of relief. Sweat had formed beneath his tightly clenched fingers.

"Have you told any lies?"

The question caught him off guard. Like everyone who lies habitually and without thinking, he held tremendous respect and fear for the truth. Something that felt almost separate from himself compelled him to give a swift, wounded response.

"Oh, no, Father, I never tell lies."

For a moment, like an ordinary person sitting on a king's throne, he savored the pride that came with his position. But as the priest started to quietly speak the usual warnings, he understood that by heroically insisting he hadn't lied, he had committed a dreadful sin—he had lied during confession.

In automatic response to Father Schwartz's "Make an act of contrition," he began to repeat aloud meaninglessly:

"Oh, my God, I am deeply sorry for having offended You...."

He had to fix this immediately—it was a terrible error—but just as his teeth clenched on the final words of his prayer, there was a sharp noise, and the slat snapped shut.

A minute later, when he stepped out into the twilight, the relief of leaving the stuffy church for an open world of wheat fields and sky delayed his full understanding of what he had just done. Rather than worrying, he took a deep breath of the fresh air and started repeating to himself again and again the words "Blatchford Sarnemington, Blatchford Sarnemington!"

Blatchford Sarnemington was his true self, and these words essentially formed a poem. When he transformed into Blatchford Sarnemington, an elegant grace radiated from him. Blatchford Sarnemington experienced magnificent, sweeping victories. When Rudolph partially closed his eyes, it signified that Blatchford had gained control over him, and as he passed by, jealous whispers filled the air: "Blatchford Sarnemington! There goes Blatchford Sarnemington."

He was Blatchford now for a while as he walked confidently homeward along the uneven road, but when the road straightened itself with paved stones to become the main street of Ludwig, Rudolph's excitement faded away and his thoughts became clear, and he felt the terror of his lie. God, naturally, already knew about it—but Rudolph kept a part of his mind where he was protected from God, where he devised the deceptions with which he frequently fooled God. Taking refuge now in this corner he thought about how he could best escape the results of his false statement.

He had to avoid communion the next day at any cost. The danger of provoking God's anger to such a degree was far too serious. He would need to drink water "accidentally" in the morning, which would make him unable to receive communion that day according to church rules. Despite how weak this plan was, it seemed like the most practical solution he could think of. He decided to accept the dangers it involved and focused on figuring out the best way to carry it out as he walked around the corner past Romberg's Drug Store and saw his father's house come into view.

Chapter 3

Rudolph's father, who worked as the local freight agent, had arrived with the second wave of German and Irish immigrants to the Minnesota-Dakota region. In theory, tremendous opportunities awaited an energetic young man in that time and place, but Carl Miller had been unable to build the kind of reputation for steady reliability with either his bosses or his workers that was crucial for success in a business with strict hierarchies. While he was somewhat crude, he was also not tough-minded enough and couldn't accept basic workplace relationships as they were, and this shortcoming made him distrustful, restless, and constantly troubled.

His two connections to the vibrant world around him were his faith in the Roman Catholic Church and his almost mystical reverence for the Empire Builder, James J. Hill. Hill embodied everything that Miller lacked—an intuitive understanding of situations, a natural feel for circumstances, the ability to sense change coming like detecting rain in the wind against one's face. Miller's thoughts dwelled endlessly on decisions that other men had made long ago, and never once in his entire life had he experienced the weight of responsibility for any meaningful choice. His tired, energetic, small frame was aging in the enormous shadow cast by Hill. For two decades he had lived in solitude with only Hill's legacy and God for company.

On Sunday morning Carl Miller woke up in the spotless silence of six o'clock. Kneeling beside his bed, he pressed his yellowish-gray hair and the thick, speckled fringe of his mustache into the pillow and prayed for several minutes. Then he pulled off his nightshirt—like others of his generation, he had never been able to tolerate pajamas—and dressed his slender, pale, smooth body in wool underwear.

He shaved. Silence filled the other bedroom where his wife lay in restless sleep. Quiet came from the screened corner of the hallway where his son's crib sat, and his son slept surrounded by his Alger books, his collection of cigar bands, his moth-eaten pennants—"Cornell," "Hamlin," and "Greetings from Pueblo, New Mexico"—and the other belongings of his personal world. From outside Miller could hear the sharp calls of birds and the buzzing activity of the chickens, and underneath it all, the deep, building click-a-tick of the six-fifteen express train heading to Montana and the green coastline beyond. Then as the cold water dripped from the washcloth in his hand he lifted his head abruptly—he had caught a sneaky sound coming from the kitchen downstairs.

He quickly dried his razor, pulled his hanging suspenders up to his shoulders, and listened carefully. Someone was moving around in the kitchen, and he could tell from the soft footsteps that it wasn't his wife. With his mouth slightly open, he hurried down the stairs and opened the kitchen door.

Standing by the sink with one hand resting on the still-dripping faucet and the other gripping a full glass of water

65

was his son. The boy's eyes, still weighed down by sleep, looked up to meet his father's gaze with a scared, accusing beauty. He stood there barefoot, his pajamas rolled up at both the knees and sleeves.

For a moment, both of them stayed completely still— Carl Miller's eyebrows lowered while his son's rose, as if they were balancing out the intense emotions that overwhelmed them both. Then the father's mustache drooped ominously until it covered his mouth, and he quickly looked around to check if anything had been moved or damaged.

The kitchen was filled with sunlight that struck the pans and turned the polished floorboards and table surface golden and clean like wheat. It served as the heart of the house where the fire blazed and the containers nested inside one another like playthings, while steam hissed continuously in a soft, delicate tone. Everything remained in its place, undisturbed—except for the tap where droplets of water continued to gather and fall with a bright gleam into the sink beneath.

"What are you doing?"

"I got really thirsty, so I thought I'd just come down and get——"

"I thought you were going to communion."

A look of intense shock spread across his son's face.

"I forgot all about it."

"Have you drunk any water?"

"No——"

As soon as the word escaped his lips, Rudolph realized it was the wrong response, but the tired, angry eyes staring at him had already revealed the truth before the boy could think to stop himself. He also understood that he should never have come downstairs; some unclear need to make his

66

story believable had driven him to leave a wet glass by the sink as proof; his honest imagination had given him away.

"Pour it out," his father ordered, "that water!"

Rudolph desperately turned the glass upside down.

"What's wrong with you, anyway?" Miller demanded angrily.

"Nothing."

"Did you go to confession yesterday?"

"Yes."

"Then why were you going to drink water?"

"I don't know—I forgot."

"Maybe you care more about being a little bit thirsty than you do about your religion."

"I forgot." Rudolph could feel the tears welling up in his eyes.

"That's no answer."

"Well, I did."

"You better watch yourself!" His father maintained a sharp, relentless, questioning tone: "If you're so absent-minded that you can't even remember your faith, then something needs to be done about it."

Rudolph broke the tense silence by saying:

"I can remember it just fine."

"First you start ignoring your religion," his father shouted, fueling his own anger, "then you'll begin lying and stealing, and after that it's reform school!"

Not even this familiar threat could make the abyss that Rudolph saw before him any deeper. He had to either confess everything now, offering his body for what he knew would be a brutal beating, or risk divine punishment by receiving the Body and Blood of Christ with sacrilege on his soul. Of the two choices, the first seemed more terrifying—

it wasn't so much the beating he feared as the savage brutality, the outlet of a powerless man, that would drive it.

"Put down that glass and go upstairs and get dressed!" his father commanded. "And when we get to church, before you take communion, you'd better kneel down and ask God to forgive you for being so careless."

Some unintended emphasis in how this command was spoken worked like a catalyst on the chaos and fear swirling through Rudolph's mind. A fierce, defiant rage surged within him, and he hurled the glass violently into the sink.

His father made a strained, raspy noise and lunged toward him. Rudolph quickly moved to one side, knocked over a chair, and attempted to get past the kitchen table. He cried out sharply when a hand grabbed his pajama shoulder, then he felt the heavy thud of a fist hitting the side of his head, followed by glancing strikes to his upper body. As he twisted and turned in his father's grip, being dragged or lifted whenever he instinctively grabbed onto an arm, feeling sharp pains and pulls, he remained silent except for several moments of hysterical laughter. Then in under a minute the hitting suddenly stopped. After a pause during which Rudolph was held tightly, and during which both of them shook violently and spoke strange, broken words, Carl Miller partly dragged and partly forced his son upstairs.

"Put on your clothes!"

Rudolph was now both frantic and shivering. His head throbbed with pain, and a long, shallow cut marked his neck where his father's fingernail had scraped him, causing him to cry and shake as he got dressed. He could see his mother standing in the doorway wearing her robe, her lined face contracting and stretching as new waves of wrinkles rippled from her neck to her forehead. Disgusted by her nervous helplessness and rudely pulling away when she attempted to dab his neck with witch-hazel, he hurriedly and breathlessly finished getting ready. Then he walked behind his father out of the house and down the road toward the Catholic church.

Chapter 4

They walked in silence, except for the moments when Carl Miller automatically acknowledged people passing by. Only Rudolph's irregular breathing disturbed the hot Sunday quiet.

His father came to a firm stop at the church door.

"I've decided you should go to confession again. Go inside and tell Father Schwartz what you did and ask for God's forgiveness."

"You lost your temper, too!" said Rudolph quickly.

Carl Miller took a step toward his son, who carefully moved backward.

"All right, I'll go."

"Are you going to do what I say?" his father demanded in a rough whisper.

"All right."

Rudolph entered the church and, for the second time in two days, stepped into the confessional booth and knelt down. The wooden panel slid open almost immediately.

"I blame myself for skipping my morning prayers."

"Is that all?"

"That's all."

A sentimental excitement overwhelmed him. Never again would he easily be able to place abstract ideals above his personal comfort and dignity. An unseen boundary had been crossed, and he had become conscious of his separation from others—conscious that this isolation affected not just those times when he was Blatchford Sarnemington but extended to his entire inner existence. Until now, such things as unrealistic dreams and small embarrassments and anxieties had been merely private thoughts, unrecognized by his public self. Now he understood instinctively that these private thoughts were his true identity—and everything else was just a polished facade and a socially acceptable mask. The demands of his surroundings had forced him onto the solitary hidden path of teenage years.

He knelt in the pew next to his father. Mass started. Rudolph knelt upright—when he was by himself he would slouch back against the seat—and savored the feeling of a keen, quiet revenge. Next to him his father prayed that God would forgive Rudolph, and also asked that his own burst of anger would be pardoned. He looked sideways at his son, and felt relieved to see that the tense, frantic expression had disappeared from his face and that he had stopped crying. The Grace of God, present in the Sacrament, would take care of the rest, and maybe after Mass everything would be better. Deep down he was proud of Rudolph, and was starting to feel genuinely sorry for what he had done, not just going through the motions.

Usually, the passing of the collection box was a major moment for Rudolph during the services. When he had no money to put in, which happened frequently, he would feel intensely embarrassed and lower his head, pretending not to notice the box so that Jeanne Brady sitting in the pew behind him wouldn't observe and realize his family's severe financial struggles. But today he looked into it with detachment as it moved past him, observing with mild curiosity the many pennies it held.

When the bell rang for communion, however, he trembled. There was no reason why God wouldn't stop his heart. Over the past twelve hours he had committed a series of deadly sins that kept getting worse, and he was now about to top them all off with a blasphemous sacrilege.

"Lord, I am not worthy for you to enter under my roof; but only say the word, and my soul shall be healed...."

There was a rustling sound in the church pews, and the worshippers made their way into the aisle with their eyes lowered and hands clasped together. Those who were more devout pressed their fingertips together to create the shape of church steeples. Carl Miller was among these more pious individuals. Rudolph walked behind him toward the communion rail and knelt down, automatically placing the napkin beneath his chin. The bell rang with a sharp sound, and the priest turned away from the altar holding the white communion wafer above the chalice:

"May the Body of our Lord Jesus Christ preserve my soul for eternal life."

A cold sweat formed on Rudolph's forehead as communion started. Father Schwartz moved down the line, and Rudolph felt increasingly sick as his heart seemed to weaken under God's will. The church appeared darker to him, and a profound silence had settled over everything, interrupted only by the indistinct murmuring that signaled the approaching presence of the Creator of Heaven and Earth. He lowered his head between his shoulders and braced himself for what was coming.

Then he felt a sharp jab in his ribs. His father was prodding him to straighten up, not to lean against the railing; the priest was just two seats away.

"May the Body of our Lord Jesus Christ preserve my soul for eternal life."

Rudolph opened his mouth. The sticky, waxy taste of the communion wafer coated his tongue. He stayed completely still for what felt like an endless stretch of time, his head tilted back, the wafer remaining undissolved in his mouth. Then his father's elbow nudged him again, startling him back to awareness, and he noticed the congregation moving away from the altar like falling leaves, returning to their seats with lowered eyes, each person alone in their communion with God.

Rudolph found himself completely alone, soaked in sweat and consumed by deadly sin. As he made his way back to his seat, the sharp clicking of his split hooves echoed loudly across the floor, and he understood that a dark poison had taken hold of his heart.

Chapter 5

"Sagitta Volante in Dei"

The beautiful little boy with eyes like blue stones and lashes that spread out from them like flower petals had finished confessing his sin to Father Schwartz—and the patch of sunlight in which he sat had shifted forward half an hour into the room. Rudolph felt less afraid now; once he had shared his story, a sense of relief had washed over him. He understood that as long as he remained in the room with this priest, God would not stop his heart, so he exhaled deeply and sat quietly, waiting for the priest to speak.

Father Schwartz's cold, watery eyes stared at the carpet pattern where sunlight revealed swastikas, flat vines without blooms, and faint traces of flowers. The hallway clock ticked relentlessly toward evening, and from the dreary room and the afternoon beyond the window came a rigid sameness, broken occasionally by the echoing sound of a distant hammer striking through the dry air. The priest's nerves were stretched to their limit, and the beads of his rosary seemed to writhe and twist like serpents across the green felt surface of his table. He couldn't recall what he was supposed to say.

Of all the things in this forgotten Swedish town, he was most conscious of this little boy's eyes—those beautiful eyes, with eyelashes that seemed to leave them reluctantly and curved back as if trying to meet them again.

For another moment, the silence continued as Rudolph waited, while the priest fought to recall something that kept slipping further and further from his memory, and the clock kept ticking in the damaged house. Then Father Schwartz looked intently at the young boy and spoke in an unusual voice:

"When many people gather in the finest locations, things start to sparkle and shine."

Rudolph jumped and quickly glanced at Father Schwartz's face.

"I said—" the priest started, then stopped to listen. "Do you hear the hammer and the clock ticking and the bees? Well, that's no good. The thing is to have a lot of people in the center of the world, wherever that happens to be. Then"—his watery eyes widened knowingly—"things go glimmering."

"Yes, Father," Rudolph agreed, feeling somewhat frightened.

"What are you going to be when you grow up?"

"Well, I was planning to become a baseball player for a while," Rudolph replied nervously, "but I don't think that's a very good goal, so I think I'll become an actor or a Navy officer."

Again the priest stared at him.

"I understand exactly what you're getting at," he said, with an intense look.

Rudolph hadn't intended anything specific, and when it was suggested that he had, he grew even more uncomfortable.

"This guy is insane," he thought, "and he terrifies me. He's looking for my help with something, and I want nothing to do with it."

"You look like everything fell apart," Father Schwartz exclaimed frantically. "Have you ever been to a party?"

"Yes, Father."

"And did you notice that everyone was dressed appropriately? That's exactly what I'm talking about. Right when you walked into the party, there was a moment when everyone looked perfectly put together. Perhaps two young girls were standing near the entrance and some boys were leaning against the railings, with bowls of flowers scattered throughout the room."

"I've been to a lot of parties," said Rudolph, feeling somewhat relieved that the conversation had shifted in this direction.

"Of course," Father Schwartz continued triumphantly, "I knew you would agree with me. But my theory is that when a large group of people gather in the finest places, things constantly go glimmering."

Rudolph found himself thinking of Blatchford Sarnemington.

"Please listen to me!" the priest commanded impatiently. "Stop worrying about last Saturday. Apostasy only leads to absolute damnation if there was previously perfect faith. Does that clear things up?"

Rudolph had no idea what Father Schwartz was talking about, but he nodded anyway, and the priest nodded back at him before returning to his mysterious preoccupation.

"Why," he exclaimed, "they have lights now as large as stars—do you understand that? I heard about one light they had in Paris or somewhere that was as big as a star. Many people had it—many cheerful people. They have all kinds of things now that you never imagined."

"Listen—" He moved closer to Rudolph, but the boy pulled back, so Father Schwartz returned to his chair and sat down, his eyes dry and burning. "Have you ever been to an amusement park?"

"No, Father."

"Well, go and visit an amusement park." The priest gestured with his hand in a vague manner. "It's something like a carnival, only much more dazzling. Visit one during the evening and position yourself at some distance from it in a shadowy spot—beneath dark trees. You'll observe a large wheel constructed of lights rotating in the sky, and an extended slide sending boats plunging down into the water. A band performing somewhere, and the scent of peanuts— and everything will sparkle. But it won't bring anything to mind, you understand. It will all simply suspend there in the darkness like a vibrant balloon—like an enormous yellow lantern mounted on a post."

Father Schwartz frowned as he suddenly thought of something.

"But don't get too close," he warned Rudolph, "because if you do, you'll only feel the heat and the sweat and the life."

All this conversation struck Rudolph as especially bizarre and frightening, particularly because this man was a priest. He remained seated there, half paralyzed with fear, his striking eyes wide open and fixed on Father Schwartz.

Yet beneath his fear, he sensed that his own personal beliefs were being validated. There existed something indescribably magnificent somewhere that bore no connection to God. He had stopped believing that God was furious with him over the initial lie, since He surely would have grasped that Rudolph had told it to enhance the beauty of the confessional, adding brightness to the drab nature of his confessions by speaking something brilliant and noble. In the instant when he had declared perfect honor, a silver banner had unfurled into the wind somewhere, and there had been the sound of creaking leather and the gleam of silver spurs, with a company of mounted soldiers awaiting daybreak on a gentle green slope. The sunlight had created points of light on their armor like the painting at home depicting the German heavy cavalry at Sedan.

But now the priest was mumbling unclear and heartbroken words, and the boy became wildly frightened. Terror suddenly entered through the open window, and the atmosphere of the room shifted. Father Schwartz collapsed abruptly to his knees, and let his body fall back against a chair.

"Oh, my God!" he cried out in a strange voice and collapsed to the floor.

Then a crushing sense of human suffering emanated from the priest's threadbare garments, mixing with the stale odor of old food lingering in the corners. Rudolph let out a piercing scream and fled the house in terror—while the broken man remained motionless on the floor, his presence saturating the room, flooding it with voices and faces until the space overflowed with repetitive echoes, reverberating with the constant, piercing sound of laughter.

Outside the window, the blue sirocco shimmered over the wheat fields, and blonde girls strolled sensually along the roads that bordered the farmland, calling out playful, thrilling words to the young men working between the rows of grain. Their legs showed through the soft cotton dresses, and the necklines of their garments were warm and moist with perspiration. For five hours now, this hot, fertile life had blazed in the afternoon heat. Night would come in three hours, and across the countryside there would be these fair-haired Northern girls and the tall farm boys lying together beside the wheat fields, beneath the moonlight.

The End

Thank You For Reading

You've Just Read a Piece of the Greatest Library Ever Rebuilt

Thank you for reading.

This book is one of thousands we're restoring, reimagining, and translating as part of the **Modern Library of Alexandria** — a global movement to preserve and share humanity's most important ideas.

What was once lost to fire and time is now rising again — not just as memory, but as living, breathing knowledge, freely accessible to all.

What You Can Do Next:

- **Keep Reading.**

  Discover more legendary works — in beautiful print, audiobook, or digital form — at LibraryofAlexandria.com.

- **Build Your Own Library.**

  Every title is available as a paperback, hardcover, or collectible boxset — at true printing cost. Craft a personal library worthy of display.

- **Spread the Light.**

  Share this book. Tell others about the movement. Help us translate every timeless work into every language, so no reader is ever left behind.

By finishing this book, you've already taken part in something extraordinary.

Join us at LibraryofAlexandria.com

Together, we're rebuilding the greatest library the world has ever known.

With appreciation,

The Modern Library of Alexandria Team

Visit:
www.libraryofalexandria.com
Or scan the code below: